ISBN 978-1-332-83531-7
PIBN 10166109

General
William Lee Davidson

Mr. President of the Guilford Battle Ground Company, Ladies and Gentlemen:

Fourth of July celebrations are usually expected to be accompanied with flights of eloquence and streams of oratory as the deeds of our ancestors and the blessings they have secured for mankind are brought to memory. Although a century and a fourth have elapsed since he of whom I speak to you gave his life as a part of the price of the independence of America, yet so little history has been written concerning his services that a simple memorial oration would be but little understood or appreciated by my audience. In order to have true history, we must first collect the "ana" or account of the individual incident or deeds of the individual. These the annalist arranges with reference to date of occurrence and then the historian is ready for his work. Comparison of events and individuals with panegyrics, etc., follow. Today I come not with an oration, but with some "ana," some annals, some history concerning my subject, and hope I may furnish a paper that will be useful to the writer and student of North Carolina history. I fear that many of our people do not appreciate the claims of the State to the glories and blessings of the Fourth of July—hail its coming with joyful acclaim and have a just pride in all that concerns it. The men of whom you shall hear today rendered their services and gave their lives to establish the Fourth of July as an important date in the calendars of the nations of the earth.

Then while we will never cease to honor the memory of the men who followed Lee and his lieutenants in 1861-'65, let us not forget the services of those who followed Washington and Greene in 1776-'81, and the blessings they purchased for us.

In most of the States there are no localities to recall events of the Revolution. The oldest inhabitant almost recollects the first house or even when the Indians left. The military monuments relate almost wholly to the Civil War. And as the father tells his son of the hero commemorated, embellishing with real or imaginary narration, he arouses and perpetuates sectional feeling and keeps alive in the youth animosity for a portion of his countrymen. With us it is different: this battlefield, Moore's Creek, Charlotte and the other places of revolutionary engagements, are object lessons in teaching patriotism. From almost every hill top in my vicinity we see King's Mountain; it aids in perpetuating the valor of our ancestors and encouraging love for the Union.

During the Civil War, when the body of the heroic grandson was interred by that of the grandfather of Revolutionary fame, pride was felt in his conduct and generations will be taught to remember it—but there was and has been no lessening of the admiration and veneration of the deeds of the grand-sire in making America a Nation.

GEN. WILLIAM LEE DAVIDSON.

Davidson's Creek, having its source a few miles north of Mooresville, in Iredell (formerly Rowan) county, flows in a southeast direction and empties into the Catawba river below Beattie's Ford, in Mecklenburg county.

Among the families that settled upon the lands of the upper portion of the creek prior to the Revolution were those of Davidson, Ramsey, Brevard, Osborne, Winslow, Kerr, Rankin, Templeton, Dickey, Brawley, Moore and Emerson. They came principally from Pennsylvania and Maryland. From the Davidsons the creek derived its name. They were generall Scotch-Irish Presbyterians and as was the custom of these people, organized themselves into a "congregation" for the promotion of religion and education.

Among the early settlers was George Davidson and family, from Lancaster county, Pennsylvania, in 1750. His youngest son, William Lee Davidson, was born in 1746. He was educated at Charlotte at the Academy, which afterwards became successively Queen's Museum and Liberty Hall, but probably attended the Centre Academy prior to coming to Charlotte. There is some confusion as to his name—whether "Lee" is properly a portion of it. He appears upon the muster rolls under both names. In his will, which is recorded in the office of the clerk of the Superior Court in Salisbury, he says: "I, William

Lee Davidson," and signs it "Wm. L. Davidson." This settles the question.

His pension and land grant for services are to William Davidson. He is not mentioned in the records as William Lee until he becomes lieutenant-colonel, October 4, 1777. So in historical matters he is both William and William Lee and cannot be restricted to either name. I think Lee was the maiden name of his mother, or some of her connection. His eldest son was called George Lee. His youngest son, born several months after his death and named for him, was called William Lee.

William Lee Davidson, after reaching his majority, made his home prior to his marriage with his cousin, Major George Davidson. He married Mary, the eldest child of John Brevard, and settled on Davidson's creek at what is now known as the McPherson place, and owned afterwards by Hon. Rufus Reid. He also owned the land upon which Davidson College is located. It was sold by his son, William Lee, to the trustees of the college in 1835.

DAVIDSON COUNTY.

In 1783, the Legislature organized the county of Davidson and named the county-seat Nashville, in honor of Generals Davidson and Nash. When Tennessee was conveyed to the United States this ceased to be a part of North Carolina, as did also Washington, Greene, Hawkins, Sullivan and Sumner counties. In 1822, the present county of Davidson was formed, as the State desired to honor his name. In 1777, the county of Nash had been organized.

DAVIDSON COLLEGE.

August 26, 1835, the Concord Presbytery resolved "that the manual labor institution which we are about to build be called Davidson College, as a tribute to the memory of that distinguished and excellent man, General William Davidson, who in the ardor of patriotism fearlessly contending for the liberty of his country, fell (universally lamented) in the battle of Cowan's Ford."

September 20, 1781, Congress enacted the following resolution:

"That the Governor and Council of the State of North Carolina be directed to erect a monument at the expense of the United States, not exceeding in value five hundred dollars, to the memory of the late Brigadier-General Davidson, who commanded the militia of the district of Salisbury in the State of North Carolina, and was killed on the first of February last, fighting gallantly for the defense of the liberty and independence of these State."

This matter was revived in Congress at different times, notably by Senator W. A. Graham in 1841 and 1842, and attention was called to it at various times by the Society of the Cincinnati and private individuals, among them Prof. W. A. Withers, of the North Carolina A. & M. College, and later by the Guilford Battle Ground Company, and an appropriation urged to execute the resolution of 1781, but not until 1902, through the labors of Hon. W. W. Kitchin, the present worthy Representative from this, the Fifth North Carolina District, in the House of Representatives of the United States Congress, was an appropriation secured. He was materially aided in its enactment by the labors of Colonel Benehan Cameron, who represented the Society of the Cincinnati, and Col. Joseph M. Morehead, the efficient president of the Guilford Battle Ground Company, to whose patriotic services much of the work of preserving and adorning this historic field is due. By means of this appropriation of five thousand dollars, this monument has been erected. *General Davidson was a citizen of Rowan (now Iredell) county, and his services are to be credited to that county and not to Mecklenburg, as is sometimes done.*

In 1848, in his message to the Legislature, Gov. Graham recommended an appropriation for monuments to Gens. Nash and Davidson, as Congress had neglected to make the necessary provision. In concluding, he said:

"It would be a fitting memorial of the patriotic services and

sacrifices of the illustrious dead and a perpetual incentive to *the living to lead such lives, and if duty demanded it, to devote themselves* to *such deaths for their country.*"

SERVICES IN THE REVOLUTION.

The commencement of hostilities in the Revolution was not similar to a riot or outbreak where one day there is order and law, and the next strife and turmoil. The aspirations of the people individually and collectively for liberty and self-government were well fertilized by the oppressive conduct of officers of the Crown and the unfriendly legislation of Parliament. The approach of the storm was visible and preparations were made for its coming. The flouring mills were the points where neighbors met. As he communicated his ideas of liberty to comrade he sowed seed in fertile ground, or watered that already germinating; the work continued until the harvest was ripe. The first organizations were in captains "beats," which were the unit of organization until "townships" were introduced in 1868, then by regiment or county, then Superior Court districts or brigade, afterwards State or Province.

COMMITTEES OF SAFETY.

The first governing bodies were Committees of Safety, and were organized in New Hanover, Mecklenburg, Rowan and perhaps other counties, as early as 1773. The county committees were generally composed of two representatives from each captain's beat. The convention, May 20, 1775, at Charlotte, was probably the Committee of Safety for Mecklenburg county. Gen. Graham, in his address at Charlotte, May 20, 1835, says these committees continued for fifteen years or more.

Subsequent to the Revolution they usually met after the election and framed instructions to Representatives in the Legislature, that he received such instruction in 1789 and 1790 when Senator. That at that time (1835) there were laws in existence that had been suggested by these committees. The journal of the Committee of Safety of Rowan county is preserved as early as August 8, 1774, and shows existence before that date.

William Davidson appears as a member September 23d, and

was probably one of the members at the organization. He is appointed a member of a committee of twenty-five to see that the resolves of the Provincial and Continental Congresses are observed. This is the first appearance of his name upon the records. At the same session he is appointed a member of a committee to cite certain persons to appear before the Committee of Safety to answer the charge of advancing the price of powder.

MILITIA SERVICE.

August 1, 1775, formation of companies of "minute men" is authorized, who shall be ready to respond immediately to the call of the committee. At this session he is mentioned as captain of militia and ordered to impress some ammunition in the possession of John Work. During this month the Provincial Congress provided for the organization of the State and he is named on the committee for Rowan county. The State simply extended the captain's beat and county organization, retaining the name Committee of Safety, except for the State, which was called Provincial Council.

September 20th, his militia company is reported as containing one hundred and eighteen men.

October 17, 1775, under the law of the Provincial Congress, he is elected a member of the Committee of Safety for the county of Rowan, the committee being now elected by the freeholders and householders of the county.

November 28th, he reported a company of minute men as organized and a committee is appointed to inspect the company and see that it is composed of "able, effective men."

In December, 1775, he served under Gen. Rutherford against the Schovelite tories in South Carolina in the "Snow Campaign," probably with his company of minute men; also in the campaign against the Cherokee Indians in the fall of 1776. (State Records, Vol. XV., p. 113.)

THE NORTH CAROLINA LINE, OR CONTINENTALS.

In August, 1775, North Carolina organized two regiments to serve "during the war." In April, 1776, in compliance with the act of Congress to furnish nine battalions "to serve during the war," four more regiments were organized, which, with the two formed the year before, six in all, constituted the nine battalions.

William Davidson was commissioned Major of the Fourth Regiment April 15, 1776.

These troops were designated the "North Carolina Line or Continentals," as distinguishing them from the militia, which retained its former organization, and was called into service by the State authorities for designated terms of service, generally three months. This distinction of troops was not observed by all the States. Massachusetts and the other New England States succeeded in having Congress to recognize nearly all their troops as Continentals, however short the term of enlistment or call to service, and thus had a large force recorded as Continentals who did not serve nearly as long as many of the North Carolina militia, and the New England States thus secured the appointment of a much larger number of general officers in the Continental force than they were justly entitled to, and obtained for their troops the benefit of the acts of the Continental Congress. The militia was under control of the State, the Continental, of Congress.

The frequent reduction of Gen. Washington's forces to inconveniently small numbers by the return home of many of the troops of the Northern States whose short terms of enlistment would expire, interfered much with its efficiency and prevented action of importance to the American cause.

This New England continental Army, except the officers, was with difficulty kept embodied after Washington assumed command during the siege of Boston, owing to short enlistments, and soon melted away when the British evacuated the city in March, 1776. Having had a short military service, they returned home to enjoy the comforts of the fireside and the appropriations of the Continental Congress.

In the campaign of 1776, the loss of the State of New York and the retreat through New Jersey of Washington with his depleted army is attributed to this cause.

Early in 1777, Congress, in order to remedy this evil, ordered the North Carolina Brigade to march to re-enforce the army of the commander-in-chief, and furnish him a force that could be depended upon for permanent and efficient service.

These troops, under Col. Martin, Gens. Howe and Moore, had "seen service" against the Schovilite tories in South Carolina; under Major-General Lee in the repulse of Clinton and Parker at Charleston, S. C., and against the Loyalists of the Cape Fear section. Gen. Moore had died in April, 1777. Gen. Howe was in command of the Department of the South. Col. Nash was promoted brigadier general and placed in command. The troops were in Charleston as late as February, but before May had assembled at Halifax and begun the march northward.

In May, 1777, Col. Alex. Martin, of the Second Regiment, writes Gen. Washington that he has reached Alexandria, Va., with the advance of the brigade; that nine battalions, with a total of forty-five hundred men, had left Halifax as reinforcements to his army; that the men who had not had smallpox would go into camp (at Georgetown) for inoculation; that Major Jethro Sumner would proceed immediately with a command of all the immunes. A report of Major Sumner's command, ten days later, shows only one hundred and sixty men. This would indicate that 4,300 men went into camp for inoculation. The number which died cannot be accurately stated. Governor Graham, in his address upon the "Life and Character of Gen. Greene" (December, 1860), states that "An extensive burial place is still recognized in that place (Georgetown) as the sepulchre of the North Carolina troops who died there of the malady." This was twenty years before the discovery of vaccination. The disease was communicated by applying the virus from one afflicted with it to the patient, and he had a genuine case of smallpox. Courage to endure the agonies of this camp was greater than that to face the enemy in battle.

The troops reached Washington's army in June at Middlebrook, New Jersey, and were organized by Gen. Nash.

There is no report of the services of this brigade as a body in the campaigns under Gen. Washington. It is only from references to service or parts of it by other officers that we procure any information. Concerning its action in the battle of Germantown in which the brigade was a part of the division of Major-General Greene, Marshall and other historians only state that Gen. Nash was killed. It is known that Col. Irwin and Capt. Turner were killed, Col. Buncombe was mortally wounded and taken prisoner and Col. Polk wounded.

Gen. Sullivan, of New Hampshire, in his report to the Governor of that State, says a North Carolina regiment, under Col. Armstrong, in conjunction with his own division, had driven the enemy a mile and a half beyond Chew's house, before the panic occurred. The North Carolina brigade was acting as a unit, and it is possible that this was the work of the entire command with Col. Armstrong conspicuously in the van. Davidson is promoted this date to Lieutenant-Colonel of the Fifth Regiment. Tradition says for gallantry in the action.

The earliest report of the strength of the brigade on the records of the United States War Department is November 11, 1777, and shows 139 officers and 1,025 men, total 1,156 present for duty.

After the battle of Brandywine, September 11, 1777, the Second and Third Regiments were consolidated and were called the Second. After the battle of Germantown, the First and Fourth were merged into the First. The Eighth Battalion was disbanded, the men in it being transferred to the Second Regiment. This would indicate severe loss in the North Carolina troops in these actions.

Davidson appears as Lieutenant-Colonel of the First in 1777 and 1780. In May, 1778, Congress ordered the consolidation of the North Carolina troops into full battalions and that the officers not needed to command these battalions should return to North Carolina to command the four additional regiments to be furnished by the State. Moon's creek, near the Virginia line, in Caswell county, on the old plank road, about midway between Danville, Va., and Yanceyville, N. C., and Halifax were named as points of rendezvous for the troops; and commissioners sent to these points to designate the officers of the respective commands. A church of the Primitive Baptists called by the name now marks the locality of Moon's

Creek encampment. The whole to assemble at Bladensburg, Maryland.

Lieutenant-Colonel Davidson assumed command of those who met at Charlotte, being joined on the march by volunteers from other points. On reaching Moon's Creek, news of the battle of Monmouth was received; that the British had gone to New York and there was no urgent need of reinforcements. Many of the men from western North Carolina took furloughs until again called to service. There was considerable dissatisfaction and some mutinous conduct on the part of some of the officers and men as to payment of bounty and fixing a definite time for service to commence. This was to be after passing the State's border.

July 18th, Col. Thackston writes Col. Hogan about sending the paymaster at once to Col. Davidson's relief, concerning which he (Davidson) had written him. Col. Davidson assumed command of those who continued in service and after these disagreements were settled, moved to Bladensburg to join the contingent that had assembled at Halifax, and thence to Washington's army. They remained with this army until November, 1779, when the North Carolina Continental Brigade was ordered to reinforce Gen. Lincoln at Charleston.

In May the Legislature had requested the brigade to be sent south. Congress replied that this was impracticable in the summer, but it would be done in the fall. The brigade then numbered seven hundred and thirty-seven efficient men. It arrived at Charleston in March. Col. Davidson having obtained, en route, a furlough to visit his family, did not report at Charleston before it was encompassed by the enemy and thus escaped capture at the surrender.

The muster rolls of the Continental Line show that the field officers of a regiment each had a company, the captains being omitted in organization of such companies. In Vol. XIV. of The State Records, page 294, there is the roll of Lieutenant-Colonel W. L. Davidson's company on April 23, 1779. It contained, after leaving the smallpox camp, 62 men; 19 of these had died; 9 were in the hospital and 32 present for duty, a death rate of 31 per cent., of dead and disabled 47 per cent.

The brigade suffered severely in the service with Gen. Washington.

It served in Pennsylvania, New Jersey and New York, going as far North as West Point (one of Davidson's men died at West Point); fought in the battle of Monmouth and shared in all the hardships of this memorable epoch of the war in that section.

The State was to supply the clothing, the national government the rations; the officers to purchase both for themselves. Both officers and men suffered severely, the arrearage of pay causing the officers to see even "harder times" than the men, as is shown by correspondence with the State authorities. A letter from Gen. Lockton McIntosh to Gov. Caswell from the camp at Valley Forge, states that no troops suffered more in the intensely cold winter of 1777-8 than did those of North Carolina in Washington's army.

In this service, although we see but little recorded mention of Col. Davidson, the esteem in which he was held by his comrades, and others familiar with military movements, shows that he was among the most efficient officers of the brigade.

I have never seen a report subsequent to that of Col. Martin in 1777, that returns more than 2,000 men. Of the 4,500 men who left Halifax in May, 1777, and the re-enforcements sent in 1778, only 737 effective men returned to North Carolina in December, 1779. The report for January, 1779, shows present 1,339, of whom 448 are sick. The Third Regiment reports 35 effective out of 464.

SERVICE IN NORTH CAROLINA MILITIA.

When Lord Rawdon in May, 1780, began his advance toward North Carolina, Gen. Rutherford, who commanded the militia of the Salisbury district, *i. e.*, of Rowan, Mecklenburg, Lincoln, Rutherford, Burke, and the counties in what is now Tennessee, called his forces into service. Some for three months, the usual length of a term of service, and some for such time as actually needed.

Col. Davidson reported to him at Charlotte for duty. Gen. Rutherford formed a battalion of light infantry (as mounted infantry were then designated) of one hundred men, and assigned him to this command. Principally by the aid of Gen. Graham's "Revolutionry Papers" we can connectedly follow his service from this time until death.

COLSON'S MILL.

When Lord Rawdon retired to Camden, he went with Gen. Rutherford to Ramsaur's Mill, where they arrived a few hours after the conflict had terminated. From here he marched with Gen. Rutherford to suppress the Tory leader Bryan in the "forks of the Yadkin." The forks of the Yadkin, as mentioned in history of this time, was not the territory between North and South Yadkin rivers, but that between the creeks east of the Yadkin, mostly in what is now Surry county. Bryan, whose force numbered eight hundred, having learned of the battle of Ramsaur's Mill and Rutherford's advance against him, hastily departed to unite with Maj. McArthur on the Pee Dee. Col. Davidson, with his command, which, according to Maj. Blount's letter to Gov. Nash, numbered 160 (Vol. XV., p. 6, State Records), being mounted, was dispatched down the west side of the Yadkin to overtake him, but the start he had and the celerity with which he moved, enabled Bryan to reach his friends without molestation. Learning that a party of Tories were at Colson's Mill (now probably Lowder's, in Stanly county), near the junction of Rocky and Pee Dee rivers, Col. Davidson, on July 21st, undertook to surprise and capture them, but his movements being discerned by the enemy, only partially succeeded; he killed three, wounded four and captured ten. He was severely wounded through the loins; attention being probably called to him by his conspicuous uniform; two of his men were also wounded. He was carried home where he remained two months.

APPOINTED BRIGADIER GENERAL.

Gen. Rutherford was wounded and captured at the battle of Camden, August 16th. Gen. H. W. Harrington, of the Fayetteville district, was assigned temporarily to the command of the Salisbury district. Gen. Sumner having been assigned to the command of the militia in service other than that of the Salisbury district, had Col. Davidson appointed to command the "horse" of his command. On August 31st, the Legislature appointed Colonel Davidson Brigadier-General of militia for the Salisbury district during General Rutherford's absence, and Major William R. Davie colonel of the cavalry. These appointments met with hearty approval in the Salisbury district, but Gen. Harrington, being offended at the appointment of Gen. Davidson, gave notice of his resignation as brigadier-general of militia so soon as the condition of affairs in his immediate command would admit, and on November 3d, tendered it to the Board of War. He complained of being deprived of command of the first brigade in the State a deserved compliment to the Salisbury district. Gen. Harrington had been an efficient officer and performed valuable services in the Fayetteville district. There was considerable jealousy between the militia and Continental officers when thrown in the same command.

Upon the reception of his commission, Gen. Davidson, having recovered from his wound, immediately repaired to Charlotte and entered upon his duties. He still, however, retained his commission of lieutenant-colonel in the Continental line. The militia were assembling to oppose the advance of Cornwallis, the rendezvous was at McCalpin's creek, seven miles from Charlotte, on the Camden road.

When Ferguson moved into Rutherford and Burke counties, Gen. Davidson ordered a force of militia to assemble at Sherrill's Ford to oppose him, the supposition being that Ferguson would cross the Catawba near the mountains, and move down the Yadkin in order to aid Cornwallis in crossing that stream. Col. Francis Locke, of Rowan, one of the most gallant and useful officers of this time, commanded at Sherrill's Ford, and was to be re-enforced by Col. Williams with the militia of Surry and other counties. Col. Locke had won the battle at Ramsaur's Mill, three months before, when sent by Gen. Rutherford on similar service.

CORNWALLIS AT CHARLOTTE.

The Yadkin had been designated as the place of battle and when Cornwallis advanced on the 25th of September, Gen. Sumner, with his command, immediately moved, not stopping until he had crossed at Trading Ford, near where the Southern Railroad now crosses. Gen. Davidson took position at Mallard Creek, eight miles from Charlotte, and committed to Col. Davie the opposition of Cornwallis' entrance to Charlotte and Davie in turn committed covering the retreat to Adjutant Graham. There seems to have been no intention to re-enforce the parties engaged in the fight, but each command was expected after engaging the enemy, to escape as best he could. An account of the gallant fight at Charlotte and the Cross Roads would too much enlarge my narrative and is well told elsewhere. Cornwallis was awaiting news from Ferguson and did not advance beyond Charlotte. Gen. Sumner did not recross the Yadkin; Gen. Davidson kept his command at Phifer's, and by detachments annoyed the expeditions sent from Charlotte into the adjacent country for provisions and supplies, and kept Cornwallis in ignorance of the movements of his allies. These forays extended entirely around Charlotte and there were engagaments almost daily, the most noted being that at McIntyre's farm, October 3d. The reports of Cornwallis and his officers testify to the gallantry of the troops and the patriotism of the Mecklenburg people in these affairs. While the militia that were called into service to oppose Ferguson were assembling at Sherrill's Ford. Colonels Cleveland, McDowell, Sevier, Shelby, Hampton, Winston, of North Carolina, and Campbell, of Virginia, of their own accord, were assembling for the same object such of their men as would answer their call.

When they had assembled about 1,500 men near Gilbertstown, Rutherford county, the question as to who was entitled to command could not be satisfactorily adjusted, as they were all colonels. On October 4th they sent Col. Joseph McDowell to Gen. Gates, asking for an officer to be sent to command the force. The following are extracts from this communication, viz.:

"As we have at this time called out our militia without any orders from the executives of our different States, and with the view of expelling the enemy out of this part of the country, we think such a body of men worthy of your attention and would request you to send a general officer immediately to take the command of such troops as may embody in this quarter. All our troops being militia and but little acquainted with discipline, we could wish him to be a gentleman and able to keep up a proper discipline without disgusting the soldiery.

"It is the wish of such of us as are acquainted with Gen. Davidson and Col. Morgan (if in service), that one of these gentlemen may be appointed to this command.

"BENJAMIN CLEVELAND,
"ISAAC SHELBY,
"ANDREW HAMPTON,
"WILLIAM CAMPBELL,
"JOSEPH WINSTON."

The North Carolina men belonged to Gen. Davidson's command and it is highly probable that he would have been sent.

In the meantime Col. Campbell, having individually the largest number of men, was given command, and on October 7th, the enemy was found and the battle of King's Mountain won before a commander was sent. Soon after this Gen. Smallwood, of Maryland, who had acted so gallantly at Camden and had been appointed Major-General or commander of the North Carolina militia in service, arrived and assumed command. Gen. Sumner was affronted at the appointment and retired from service for a time, or until the arrival of Gen. Greene. We have at this time quite a chapter of dissatisfaction on account of promotions. Harrington vs. Davidson, Caswell and Sumner vs. Smallwood, and Smallwood vs. Baron Stueben, if he should be placed over him.

The time for which the militia had been called in service expired in November. Gen. Gates had been relieved of the command of the Southern army and his successor, Gen. Greene, had arrived at Charlotte December 3d. Early in December Gen. Davidson ordered into service another detail of militia for three months. It seems to have been Gen. Rutherford's plan to have had his regiments divided into "details" to be called into service in succession, while in some commands when a call to service was issued, first volunteers were called for to fill it, and what was lacking in volunteers, was obtained by draft. One detail had been sent to Charleston; another had been called to meet the first advance of Cornwallis; now a third is needed to be in readiness when he again enters the State.

DAVIDSON'S PLAN OF CAMPAIGN.

Before the arrival and assumption of command of Gen. Greene, November 27th, Gen. Davidson wrote a private note to Col. Alex. Martin suggesting a plan of campaign in opposition to Cornwallis:

NOTE TO COL. MARTIN.

'SIR:—By this time you may be acquainted with the position the army is to take for the present. In the meantime it appears to me that a proper exertion of the militia of my district might greatly injure if not totally ruin the British army. I have been deliberating on this matter some time and submit my plan to your consideration, and hope that you will endeavor to present it or something that will be more eligible. My scheme is to send Gen. Morgan to the westward with his light troops and riflemen; one thousand volunteer militia, which I can raise in twenty days, and the refugees from South Carolina and Georgia to join, which will make a formidable body of desperadoes, the whole to be under Morgan's direction, and proceed immediately to Ninety-Six and prossess ourselves of the western parts of South Carolina, at the same time the main army to move down to the wax haws, which will oblige the enemy to divide (which will put them quite in our power), or vacate the present posts and collect to one point, in which case we can command the country, cut off their supplies and force them to retreat and fight the militia in their own way. The messenger waits. I have neither time nor room to make further observations. I think the scheme practicable and certain of success, unless the enemy be re-enforced. Favor me with your opinion on this matter, and believe me, dear sir.

"Your very obedient and honorable servant,

"Wm. Davidson.

"N. B.—This comes to you in a private capacity." (State Records, XIV., p. 759.)

As Gen. Davidson's troops were all infantry, about January 1st he proposed to Adjt. Joseph Graham, who had already served one term or three months, although exempt for three years on account of nine months' service in the Continental line, and who had just recovered from wounds received at Charlotte September 26th, to enlist a body of cavalry, promising him such rank as the number enlisted would entitle him to. In a few weeks he had fifty-five men, only three of whom were married, embodied, and he was commissioned captain.

OPPOSING CORNWALLIS.

Gen. Greene, in opposing Cornwallis' second advance into North Carolina, disposed his forces as follows: Gen. Huger with the Continentals at Cheraw, S. C., on the east; Gen. Morgan with Howard and Col. William Washington's cavalry and some North Carolina militia under Col. Joseph McDowell, near Broad river, on the west; for a central force, connecting these and prepared to act with either as occasion might require, he relied upon the militia of Rowan and Mecklenburg, under Gen. Davidson. The militia of these counties from the formation of committees of safety until the close of the war, while answering in full proportion all calls for troops for the line or militia service beyond the State, seem to have regarded themselves as always ready to answer calls to service in their own locality, claiming no exemptions to which any might be entitled on account of any previous service. They only asked that the call should be for fighting and not for ordinary camp duty; as soon as the fight was over they return home with or without leave. The history of the Revolution shows no history of greater valor and patriotism.

At the battle of Cowpens, January, 1781, Gen. Morgan defeated Tarleton, and by death wounds and capture, deprived

Cornwallis of the service of one-fifth of the most valuable of his regular troops. Cornwallis, in his forward movement, would have to cross the Catawba; arrangements were made to annoy and injure him while so doing, and this duty was assigned to Gen. Davidson and his North Carolina militia. Gen. Greene seems to have had no intention of a battle with Cornwallis; he ordered Gen. Huger, who commanded the Continentals at Cheraw, to retreat to Guilford Court House, which he himself proceeded to do, and when he joined him there continued his journey across the Dan.

Gen. Davidson made his arrangements at the respective fords on the Catawba river; pickets of cavalry were placed at Tuckaseege, Toole's and Cowan's Fords. Col. John Williams, of Surry, with two hundred men at Tuckaseege; Capt. Potts, of Mecklenburg, at Toole's, with seventy; Lieutenant Thomas Davidson, of Mecklenburg, at Cowan's, with twenty-five. It was supposed that the crossing would be at Beattie's Ford, the best crossing on the river, and on the main line of travel in passing through this section. Here were assembled the Orange County militia, under Col. Farmer, and the Mecklenburg under Col. Thomas Polk, and some of the Rowan men. Gen. Davidson made his headquarters at this point. Gen. Greene having notified him that he desired to see Gen. Morgan and Col. Washington at Beattie's Ford, dispatched his brother-in-law, Ephraim Davidson, then only a lad, to notify them. On January 31st, all parties had arrived at the appointed place within ten minutes. After an interview of half an hour they separated. The enemy appeared on the opposite bank during the conference. In the North Carolina Booklet for April,, 1906, is a detailed account of the battle of Cowan's Ford, hence I omit particulars of it. Gen. Davidson, by the aid of Graham's cavalry, who frequently crossed the river, kept well posted as to the position of the enemy. Gen. Greene suggested that the appearance at Beattie's Ford was probably a ruse and that Cornwallis would pass Tarleton over the river during the night at some private ford and attack Davidson in the rear at the point selected for crossing. Patrols were ordered up and down the river between the fords, to be kept moving all night. Gen. Davidson, after Greene's departure, remarked to Capt. Graham that "This was Gen. Greene's first view of the Catawba, but he seemed to know as much about it as those who were reared on it."

Gen. Davidson had probably learned through friends that Cowan's had been selected as the point of crossing, and moved Col. Polk's force and Graham's cavalry to this point, where they arrived after dark and spent the night near by. Information received led them to think that the horse ford would be chosen as the route for the crossing. This information was probably gained from persons who had heard the inquiries of the officers as to the fords. The horse ford was much the best bottom and shallower water, while the wagon ford was not half the length. The horse ford reaches the bank a quarter of a mile below the wagon ford.

GEN. DAVIDSON KILLED.

Gen. O'Hara, supported by Tarleton, had been chosen as the force to cross at Cowan's. The British entered the water; O'Hara's infantry in front, with poles to steady themselves against the swift current, Tarleton's cavalry following. About the time O'Hara moved, Webster had his men to go into the river at Beattie's Ford and fire their guns; also opened with his artillery; made a feint as if he were going to cross in order to detract attention from Cowan's. As soon as Lieutenant Davidson's pickets discovered the enemy, they opened fire. They were re-enforced by Graham's men, dismounted, who joined in the firing. Gen. Davidson, hearing the firing, repaired immediately to Col. Polk's command and ordered them to move up to the wagon ford. He directed Capt. Graham to give place to Polk's men and to mount his men, form on the ridge in the rear and be prepared to meet any attack as Gen. Greene had suggested. The enemy reached the bank before many of Polk's men got into position, and securing the crossing, immediately loaded, and advancing up the bank, began firing. Gen. Davidson ordered a retreat for 100 yards down the river. The firing became so heavy that his command fell back fifty yards farther. He ordered his men to take shelter behind the trees and renew the battle. The enemy were advancing in line, firing slowly,

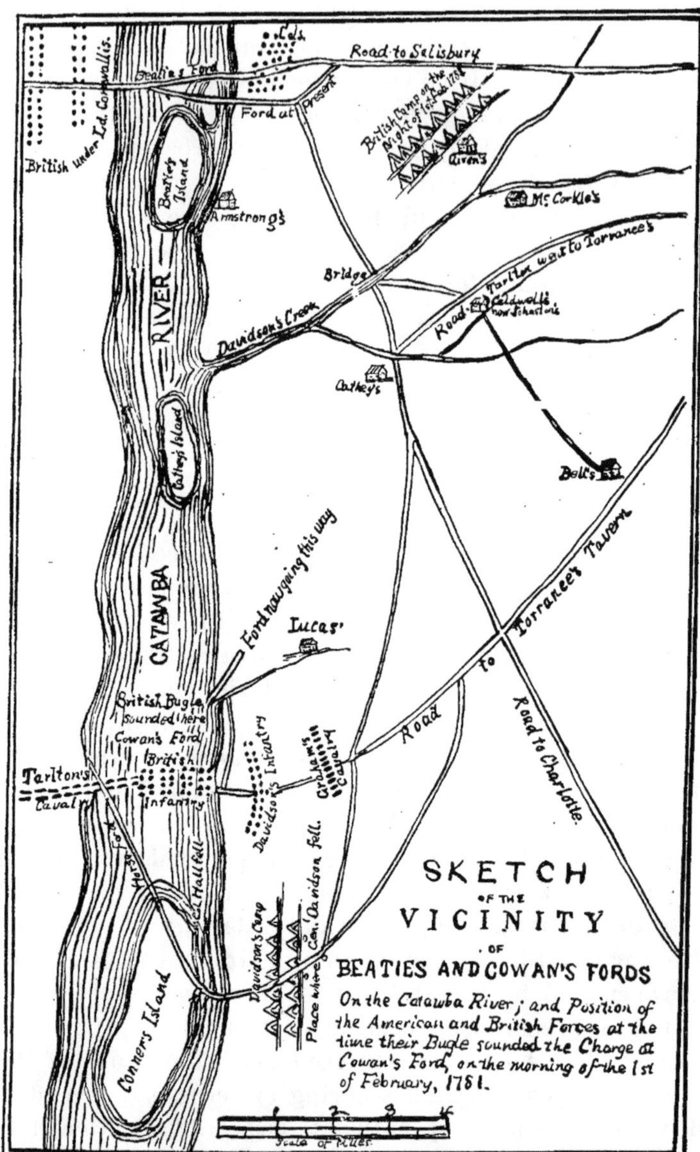

From Gen. J. P. Graham and His Revolutionary Papers.

when Gen. Davidson was shot, being instantly killed. The infantry immediately dispersed, going through the bushes to avoid the enemy's cavalry. Capt. Graham brought off his command in order.

Gen. Davidson was shot through the left breast by a small rifle ball. As the British carried muskets, this is supposed to have been done by a Tory, who acted as pilot to the enemy in crossing the river. The enemy did not discover Gen. Davidson's body. They buried the three other Americans who were killed at the river, and all of their dead, including Maj. Hall. He fell down the river from the ford and they moved up the river on leaving. Gen. Davidson's horse, after he fell, went to the house of Maj. John Davidson, where Jos. G. Davidson now lives, near Toole's Ford. Major. David Wilson, who was with Gen. Davidson when he fell, assisted by his pastor, Rev. Mr. McCaul, and Richard Harry, took the body to the residence of Samuel Wilson, where it was prepared for burial and that night interred at Hopewell church, some three miles away, by torchlight, as the night was very dark. It is stated by some writers that the body, before recovery, had been stripped of its clothing, but this is very improbable. His sword was recovered and is now preserved at Davidson College. If the clothing had been taken, the sword would not have been left. His grave is still known, although unmarked by memorial stone. Mrs. Davidson was informed of the General's death at her home some eight or ten miles away, and her neighbor, George Templeton, whose descendants still live in the community near Mooresville, accompanied her to the burial.

Thus at the age of thirty-four years fell one of the most useful men that North Carolina furnished in the struggle for independence, after more than six years service in various positions, in each of which he met the demands of the occasion.

Light Horse Harry Lee says of him in his "Memoirs:"

"The loss of Brigadier Davidson would have been always felt in any stage of the war. It was particularly detrimental in its effects at this period, as he was the chief instrument relied upon by Greene for the assembly of the militia, an event all important at this crisis and anxiously desired by the American general. The ball passed through his breast and he instantly fell dead. This promising soldier was thus lost to his country in the meridian of life and at a moment when his services would have been highly beneficial to her. He was a man of popular manners, pleasing address, active and indefatigable; devoted to the profession of arms and to the great cause for which he fought. His future usefulness may be inferred from his former conduct. The Congress of the United States in gratitude for his services and in commemoration of their sense of his worth, passed suitable resolutions."

He made his will December, 1780, appointing his father-in-law, John Brevard, his bother-in-law, Wm. Sharpe, and John Dickey executors. Only Dickey and Sharpe acted, and in 1783 presented a memorial to the Legislature of the State for settlement of amount due for his services. This was ordered paid. The matter is again referred to in the session of 1790, November 29th, and of 1792. H. J. December 5th. When he was appointed brigadier-general of the militia, he still retained his position in the "line" as Gen. Rutherford would when exchanged, assume the command of the militia. In December, 1780, Gen. Sumner was ordered by Congress to report the supernumerary officers of the Continental line who were unnecessary on account of the reduced number of the force, and could be dropped. Gen. Sumner, in making his report January 27, 1781, to Gen. Greene, regrets that the country is to lose the valuable services of these officers. He includes Gen. Davidson in the list, as he states at his request. (State Records, Vol. XV., p. 501.)

On December 31, 1780, his connection with the North Carolina Continentals ended, but the dropped officers, or their widows, were to receive half pay until seven years after the close of the war. (101, Vol. XV.)

DAVIDSON'S BRIGADE AFTER HIS DEATH.

As this paper is intended to be historical a short notice of Gen. Davidson's Brigade after his death is annexed. A full account of this is given in Gen. Graham's Revolutionary Papers. They did not conclude that as the enemy had left their borders they would return home and leave him to the attention of those whom he might next visit, but being unable to stop his advance, formed to annoy his rear and serve as best they could wherever needed until their term of service expired. They assembled at Harris' Mill, on Rocky river, the next day and started in pursuit of the enemy. On the 11th of February at Shallow Ford they requested Gen. Andrew Pickens, of South Carolina, to assume command, as there was no general officer of this State present, and Major James Jackson, of Georgia, afterwards Governor of that State, was appointed brigade major, or as we say now adjutant general. There were seven hundred of Davidson's men and some thirty or forty refugees from South Carolina and Georgia. .Gen. Pickens continued in command until the expiration of the three months' term of his men early in March and just before the battle of Guilford Court House.

Gen. Pickens, being from South Carolina, has caused historians to credit these troops to that State. Gen. Pickens was a brave and efficient commander and his association with the North Carolina troops entirely pleasant, but the troops were North Carolinians and their services should be credited to the State. On February 18th, preparations for battle were made upon the alarm of "Tarleton is coming." It proved to be Light Horse Harry Lee with his legion, whose, uniform—dark green—was the same as that of Tarleton. This was the first intelligence that Gen. Greene had of the whereabouts of Davidson's command or that Pickens had that Greene had recrossed the Dan. The brigade then served with Gen. Greene until the term of service expired early in March, participating in the engagement at Clapps, Whitsell or Hart's Mills, Pyle's massacre and other points. Some of them remained longer but the last departed for home March 10.

A query, concerning which, the students of history can employ themselves is: whether the seven hundred men of Davidson's brigade, nearly all of whom had seen service in two or three campaigns, would not have been more valuable in the battle of Guilford Court House than those of the raw troops of Butler and Eaton; and if it was not a mistake in Gen. Greene to defer battle awaiting the arrival of the latter until Pickens (or Davidson's) men had been disbanded.

PAPER RELATING TO GEN. DAVIDSON'S SERVICES.

ROLL OF W. L. DAVIDSON'S COMPANY.

Pension Office. Book entitled "North Carolina Miscellaneous Rolls." Not paged.

Roll of Lieutenant Col. Davidson's Company on the 23rd of April, 1779: (Copied from Orderly Book of Sergeant Isaac Rowel.)

First Lieutenant—Edward Yarborough.

Second Lieutenant—Reuben Wilkerson.

Sergeant—Isaac Rowel, John Horton, John Godwin.

Corporal—Jesse Baggett, Dempsy Johnson, James Thorp.

Privates—Adam Brevard, Samuel Boyd, James Boyd, Uriah Bass, Bird, Cornett, Timothy Morgan, Joseph Furtrell, Wm. Grant, Daniel Parker, Council Bass, Fifer, Barny Johnson, Richard Sumner, Sothey Manly, Booth Newton, Pioneer, Wm. Scott, Pioneer, Lemon Land, Waiter, Hardy Short, John Norwood, Joshua Reams, Buckner Floyd, Wm. Hatchcock, Solomon Deberry, Thomas Wiggins, Wm. Wilkinson, John Wilson, David Journekin, Samuel Davis.

Left at Hospital—Barnaby Murrel, Drummer, Wm. Moore, Charles Gibson, James Robards, Sterling Scott, Waiter, Hardy Portiss, Wm. Smith, Isham Jones, Lithro Lane, left at Trenton, Johsua Lewis, Robert Monger, Wm. Gray, Jos. Ward, Isaac Gunns, Chas. Thompson, John Carter, and James Goodson, died at New Windsor Hospital, Maryland; John Feasley, died at West Point; Henry Short and Caleb Woodard, at Robertson's Hospital and Matthew Murrel, Andrew Rowell, Peter Valentine, Josiah Measley, Benj. Brittle, John Clark, John Batliss and John Floyd, at Philadelphia Hospital. (State Rec., XIV., page 294.)

DAVIDSON'S COMMISSION AS BRIGADIER GENERAL.

"State of North Carolina.

"In the House of Commons, 31st August, 1780.

"Mr. Speaker and Gentlemen:

"Whereas from the late captivation of General Rutherford

by the enemy in South Carolina the militia of Salisbury district is in a manner left destitute of a general officer to command them; therefore

"Resolved, That William Lee Davidson be appointed Brigadier General of the militia for said district until the return of General Rutherford from captivity.

"THOMAS BENBURY,
Speaker Commons."

"In the Senate 31st August, 1780, concurred with

"ALEX MARTIN,
"Speaker Senate."

COUNCIL OF WAR.

At a Council of War held at the camp at New Providence, in the State of North Carolina, the 25th of November, 1780, consisting of the Commander-in-Chief, Major-General Smallwood, Brigadier-General Huger, Brigadier-General Morgan, Brigadied-General Davidson, Colonel Kosciusko, Chief Engineer, Colonel Buford, Lieutenant-Colonel Howard, Lieutenant-Colonel Washington.

The Council being assembled the Commander-in-Chief acquaintes them that: The want of provisions and forage in the camp, the advanced season of the year, the almost total failure of the herbage, the entire want of a magazine of salt meat and the uncertainty of providing it, the increasing sickness and the unwholesome situation of the camp, the want of any proper accommodation of the sick, the want of hospotal stores and proper comforts necessary for sick and diseased soldiers, the probability of reinforcement being sent from the enemy at New York, the invasion of Virginia, and the apparent prospect of Sir Harry Clinton's supporting that invasion and commanding a co-operation with Cornwallis, the State and strength of the army compared with that of the enemy, and the expediency of reinforcement coming to our army are the motives which induced him to assemble this Council of War and request their opinion of the movement and the position that the army ought to take in the present circumstances.

The Council having fully deliberated upon the matter before

them and the question being put of what position the troops ought to take, whether at or near Charlotte or at the Waxhaws or in the neighborhood, the junior member, Lieutenant Col. Washington, gave it as his opinion that at or near Charlotte should be the present position of the army to which every other member of the Council consented but Gen. Smallwood, who was for the army's moving to the Waxhaws, taking post there for three weeks, and then returning to Charlotte.

(Signed:)

H. Walter Gates,
W. Smallwood,
Isaac Huger,
Daniel Morgan,
Wm. Davidson,
Thad Kosciusko,
("Thadeus of Warsaw.")
N. Buford,
J. E. Howard,
Wm. Washington.

—. —. Clovis, Richmond, Sec'y. to Gen. Gates.

To Gen. Gates:

Camp Colo. Phifer's, October 6, 1780.

The enemy is still confined to Charlotte. The small rifle companies I have kept hanging upon their lines have been of service in checking their foraging parties. They are probably 1.800 strong, including those Loyalists they have received recruited in the Southward. Besides these they have some unformed tories who follow the fortunes of the army; rather a dead weight than a benefit.

A Col. Ferguson, in the British service, has by a variety of means been pernicious to our interests in the west of both the Carolinas. There has such a force taken the field against him as will probably rid us of such a troublesome neighbor. As the main strength of the British in the Southern States seems collected in Charlotte I have adopted every measure in my power to annoy them.

WM. DAVIDSON.

Dispatch to Gen. Sumner:

October 8th, 1780.

I have the pleasure to enclose you a large packet of dispatches taken yesterday at McCalpin's creek on the way to Camden by a small party of my brigade. A detachment of 120 horses under Rutledge and Dixon almost surrounded Charlotte yesterday, attacked a pickquet at Col. Polk's mill and at a certain Mr. Elliott's brought a sentry of eight Tories who are now on their way to you. A small party of riflemen brought off fifty horses from the Tories at Col. Polk's plantation last night. Dixon lost one man killed.

I have the honor to be, etc., etc.

WM. DAVIDSON.

Vol. XIV., p. 644.

Camp Rocky River, Oct. 10, 1780.

Sir:—I have two detachments of Cavalry and Infantry, each on the enemy's line. A considerable quantity of powder was secured some time ago within four miles of Charlotte, which I knew nothing of until Sunday evening. 13 cags were brought off that night, and the remainder sixteen have this moment arrived safe, which I will forward immediately. Pray let me know if his Lordship's figures have been deciphered yet. I find he is determined to surprise me and I am as determined to disappoint him. Inclosed you have a draft of the enemy's lines which was sent to me by Col. P——k, whilst a prisoner. I believe it may be depended on. Col. Davie is very poorly.

I am etc., etc.,

WM. DAVIDSON."

N. B.—Gen. Graham in an address at Charlotte, May 20th, 1835, says this powder had been moved from Camden to Charlotte in the fall of 1779, and was guarded by the students of the Academy; that when there was expectation of the enemy advancing several of the signers of the Mecklenburg Declaration on a day agreed upon came with sacks in which they filled the powder and conveyed it to places of safety, they appeared like boys going to mill. It was concealed in separate places—afterwards afforded a reasonable supply—not much was damaged and the enemy got none. (N. C. Booklet, January 1906.)

Tuesday evening a small party of my infantry fell in with two wagons on their way from Camden within two miles of Charlotte. They killed two men, took and brought off the wagons, horses and portmanteaus with officers' baggage. (Page 786.)

To Gen. Sumner:

October 11, 1780.

Nothing new from Charlotte. Had we more men we could make their forage cost them dear. The appearance of 50 men yesterday caused 400 to return without a handful. Inform Gov. Nash.

CPSIA information can be obtained
at www.ICGtesting.com
Printed in the USA
BVHW04s1407160818
524720BV00012B/633/P